Look around a

ROMAN VILLA

Jane Bingham

W

FRANKLIN WATTS
LONDON•SYDNEY

First published in 2007 by Franklin Watts

Franklin Watts
338 Euston Road
London NW1 3BH

Franklin Watts Australia
Level 17/207 Kent Street, Sydney, NSW 2000

Produced by Arcturus Publishing Limited,
26/27 Bickels Yard, 151–153 Bermondsey Street, London SE1 3HA

Series concept: Alex Woolf
Editor and picture researcher: Alex Woolf
Designer: Ian Winton
Plan artwork: Phil Gleaves
Consultant: Martin Henig

Picture credits:
AKG Images: cover foreground and 9 (Richard Booth).
Art Archive: 4 (Bardo Museum, Tunis / Dagli Orti), 6 (Musée Luxembourgeois Arlon, Belgium / Dagli Orti), 7
(Musée Luxembourgeois, Arlon, Belgium / Dagli Orti), 8 (Dagli Orti), 10 (Dagli Orti), 11 (National Museum,
Bucharest / Dagli Orti), 12 (Museo della Civilta Romana, Rome / Dagli Orti), 13 (Dagli Orti), 14
(Archaeological Museum, Naples / Dagli Orti), 15 (Siritide Museum, Policoro / Dagli Orti [A]), 16
(Archaeological Museum, Beirut / Dagli Orti), 17 (Dagli Orti), 18 (Dagli Orti), 19 (Dagli Orti), 20
(Archaeological Museum, Naples / Dagli Orti [A]), 21 (Provinciaal Museum G M Kam, Nijmegen, Netherlands
/ Dagli Orti), 23 (Musée du Louvre, Paris / Dagli Orti), 24 (Archaeological Museum, Milan / Dagli Orti), 25
(Dagli Orti), 26 (Musée Romain, Nyon / Dagli Orti), 27 (Museo della Civilta Romana, Rome / Dagli Orti), 29
(Museo della Civilta Romana, Rome / Dagli Orti).
Bridgeman Art Library: 22 (Museo Archeologico Nazionale, Naples).
Arcturus Publishing Ltd: 28.

A CIP catalogue record for this book is available from the British Library.

Dewey Decimal Classification Number: 937

ISBN 978 0 7496 7196 9

Printed in China

Franklin Watts is a division of Hachette Children's Books.

CONTENTS

LOOK AROUND A ROMAN VILLA

Welcome to your tour of a Roman villa. During your visit, you will see the villa's grand public spaces and its private rooms. You will relax in the shady garden, take a dip in the baths and enjoy a splendid banquet. You will also take a look behind the scenes and see the servants hard at work.

Fishbourne Palace

The Roman villa that you will explore is based on Fishbourne Palace in southern England. This luxury home was built around the year 80 CE. The villa's owner was one of the most important people in Roman Britain. He used his country villa as a place to relax with his family, and also invited many guests to stay.

Country homes

Many wealthy Romans owned a villa in the country, where they went to escape from the stresses of city life. Roman villas were large and comfortable, and were surrounded by farming land. A large staff of servants kept the house in order, prepared all the meals, and ran the farm. Some of these servants were slaves who belonged to the villa's owner, but others were free men and women who were paid for their work.

Villas were built all over the Roman Empire. This mosaic shows a villa in North Africa.

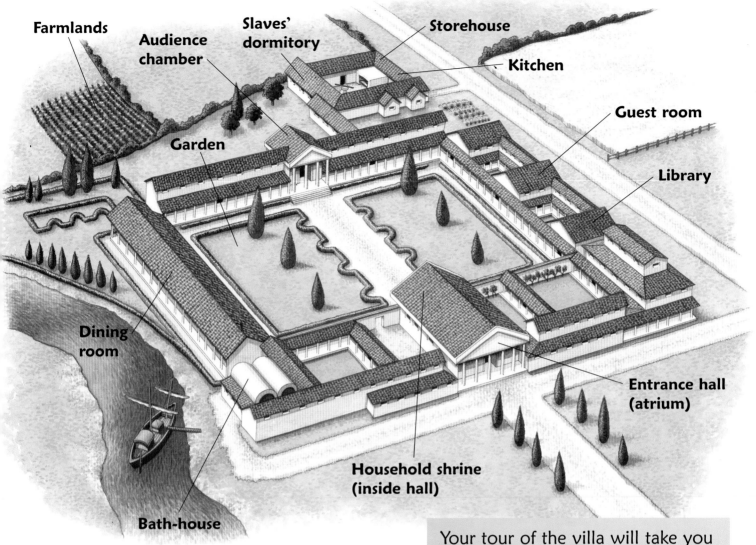

Farmlands

Audience chamber

Slaves' dormitory

Storehouse

Kitchen

Guest room

Garden

Library

Dining room

Bath-house

Household shrine (inside hall)

Entrance hall (atrium)

Your tour of the villa will take you to all the areas shown on this plan.

Changing styles

The early Roman villas were simple farmhouses. However, as Rome grew richer, people had more money to spend on their country homes. By the first century CE, some very wealthy Romans were building villas with hundreds of rooms. These elegant palaces had under–floor heating and were decorated with fine mosaics and wall paintings. They also had beautiful gardens, filled with pools, fountains and statues.

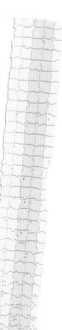

The writer Pliny loved to escape from Rome to his country villa. In this letter, Pliny invites his friend to stay with him in his villa.

You are surprised that I am so fond of my villa, but you will cease to wonder when I tell you about its beauty, the advantages of its position, and its wonderful view of the sea.

Pliny the Younger, Letters, 1st century CE

FARMLANDS

As you approach the villa, you start to notice people working in the fields. For several miles around the house, the countryside has been cleared for farmland. There are meadows where cows, goats and sheep are grazing. You also notice the neatly planted fields of wheat, cabbages, carrots and beans and the orchards of apple trees. Closer to the villa are pens for pigs, paddocks for horses, and yards for chickens and geese.

Farmlands

Making money

The farmlands of a Roman villa had a double purpose. The farm had to supply enough food for the villa's owners and his family and guests. But the villa's owner also expected his farm to make a profit. Most of the food produced on the farm was taken to market to be sold.

This simple machine is a modern reconstruction of a Roman harvester. It would have been pushed by an ox.

Running the farm

Goatherds, swineherds and cowherds looked after the animals in the meadows, while field hands were responsible for sowing, growing and harvesting vegetables, fruit and crops. The field hands worked in gangs, and each gang had a foreman who made sure that everyone was working hard. The farm's ducks, geese and hens were usually fed by women, who gave the animals scraps from the kitchens. Female servants also milked the cows and goats, and made cheese in the dairy.

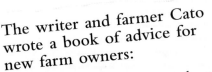
KITCHEN – SEE PAGES 24–25

All the servants on a Roman farm had to follow the orders of the farm manager. He checked that the jobs were done on time, and sent food to market to be sold. The manager kept very careful accounts, which he had to show to the villa's owner.

The writer and farmer Cato wrote a book of advice for new farm owners:

As soon as you are clear how the business stands ... send for the manager and ask him how much of the work is finished, how much remains ... and how it is with the wine, the grain and everything else.

Cato, On Agriculture,
1st century BCE

Scenes of country life have been carved on this Roman pillar from the second century CE. The upper scene shows farmers selling fruit at a market. In the lower scene, labourers are digging the land.

ENTRANCE HALL

At the front of the villa is the grand entrance hall, or atrium. Here you will find the villa's owner and his wife waiting to welcome you. The atrium is a very pleasant place to recover from a hot and tiring journey. Settle down for a chat on one of the marble seats beside the long, shallow pool, known as the *impluvium*.

Entrance hall

A shady corner of the atrium in the Villa of Poppea, Italy. The villa was built in the first century BCE.

Fresh air and water

The Romans enjoyed being out of doors, but they tried to stay in the shade as much as possible. They loved to look at cool water and green gardens, and listen to the soothing sound of fountains. Roman villas had shady, covered walkways built around gardens and courtyards. In some villas, the roof of the atrium had a large opening to let in air and sunlight. The opening was directly above the *impluvium*, so the pool could be filled with fresh rainwater.

GARDEN – SEE PAGES 12–13

Villa owners liked to decorate their homes in the latest style. At Fishbourne, the walls and ceilings of the atrium were painted with bold panels of red, purple and blue, while the floor was covered in a striking black-and-white mosaic.

Mosaic floors

Mosaic floors were laid in Roman villas, temples and palaces. They were made from thousands of tiny cubes of stone, marble or pottery. These cubes, known as *tesserae*, were pressed into wet cement to create a hard-wearing surface. The subjects shown in Roman mosaics range from simple geometric designs to elaborate scenes. Many mosaics feature stories from Roman history or legend. Others show scenes from daily life, such as farmers at work.

Pliny had a seaside villa with a large hall that had many doors and windows. It had wonderful views on all four sides.

On every side of the hall there are folding doors and windows so you have a view from three sides of the sea. From the back, you see the courtyard and the woods and distant mountains beyond.

Pliny the Younger, Letters, 1st century CE

ROMAN WALL PAINTINGS
– SEE PAGE 17

This dramatic mosaic floor comes from Fishbourne Palace. It features Cupid, the Roman god of love, riding on the back of a dolphin.

HOUSEHOLD SHRINE

Household shrine (inside atrium)

Before you leave the atrium, remember to stop at the household shrine, which is set into one of the walls. This small altar is known as the *lararium* and is dedicated to the villa's guardian spirits, or *lares*. You will see some small carved figures of the *lares* standing on the altar. In front of the *lararium* there are gifts of flowers, food and wine – offerings from the family. You can add your own gifts and ask the spirits to guard over you while you are in their home.

Household spirits

Each Roman family had their own *lares*, who kept them safe and represented the spirits of their family's ancestors. Even the poorest families had some simple clay figures of their household spirits. Whenever a family moved house, they took their *lares* with them. Every day, the family held short prayers at the *lararium* and gave small offerings to their household spirits. On special days, such as weddings or birthdays, families held elaborate services and gave precious gifts to the *lares*.

This *lararium* is from a Roman villa in Italy. Four carved figures of household spirits stand on the altar.

Gods and goddesses

As well as praying to household spirits, the Romans also worshipped a large number of gods and goddesses. Two very popular gods were Mars, the god of war, and Venus, the goddess of the hunt. Statues of Mars and Venus were often placed on the altar of the *lararium*, alongside the figures of the *lares*. People prayed to Mars to protect their home and asked Venus to look after their land.

In Cato's book of advice for new villa owners, he reminds them to visit the household shrine:

Each time you visit the farm, you must first greet the Lares of the Household.

Cato, On Agriculture, 1st century BCE

This bronze figure of a dancing household spirit carries a drinking horn – a sign of plenty. An elaborate figure like this would have come from a wealthy home.

Festivals

Throughout the year, the Romans held festivals in honour of their gods. Many of these festivals were connected with country events, such as planting or harvest time. At these times, all the people in a country villa joined in the singing, feasting and dancing. One of the most popular festivals was Saturnalia. At this midwinter feast, masters waited on their slaves, people exchanged gifts, and a 'king' was chosen to rule over the merrymakers.

GARDEN

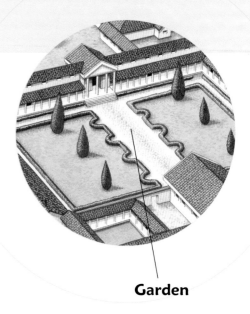

Garden

After you leave the atrium, a servant leads you across the garden to your room. As you walk along the garden's central path, notice the neatly trimmed hedges on either side. Enjoy the sound of splashing water in the marble fountains, and smell the perfume of roses and sweet-smelling herbs.

Roman gardens

The Romans loved gardens and gardening. Most Roman houses had a garden, where people could relax. Even poor people in city apartments liked to keep plants in pots and window boxes. Roman gardens were usually laid out in a formal pattern with neat hedges and flowerbeds and evergreen trees. They often included statues, pools and fountains. Roses were one of the Romans' favourite flowers. They also loved lilies and poppies, and a stiff-leaved plant called acanthus.

Not all Roman gardens were stiff and formal. This charming wild garden scene was painted on the wall of a villa in Rome.

Some Roman gardens were incredibly grand. The gardens surrounding the Emperor Hadrian's villa at Tivoli featured large pools and waterfalls, and buildings in Roman, Greek and Egyptian styles. Many villa gardens, such as the one at Fishbourne, were surrounded by a covered walkway called a *peristyle*. Slaves could use the *peristyle* to reach all the different parts of the villa without walking through any private rooms.

The grounds of this ruined villa have been planted in the Roman style. The formal garden features neatly trimmed hedges and small bushes.

Some Roman gardeners showed off their skill by cutting hedges into fantastic shapes. Here, Pliny describes some amazing hedges:

Many paths are separated by a box hedge cut into a thousand different shapes and names. Sometimes the letters spell the name of the master of the villa, or the name of the garden designer.

Pliny the Younger, Letters, 1st century CE

Herbs and vegetables

As well as enjoying their formal garden, many Romans kept a second garden for growing vegetables and herbs. In towns, these gardens were often outside the city walls. People grew a range of vegetables, such as marrows, cucumbers and lettuce, as well as onions and garlic to flavour their food. Many Romans grew herbs to use in their cooking and also to make into medicines. Rosemary, thyme and mint were popular herbs for flavouring food. Stinging nettles were eaten as a vegetable, and made into a hair tonic for balding men!

ROMAN COOKING – SEE PAGE 25

GUEST ROOM

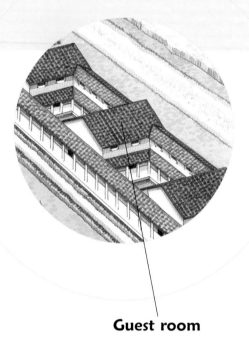

Guest room

Now it is time to settle into your room. As an important visitor, you have been given a special guest room – one of a set of rooms grouped around a small private garden. As well as a sleeping couch, your room contains a wardrobe and some small tables and chests. After you have rested, you will need to change your clothes and prepare to meet the other guests. Luckily, your personal slaves are very skilled at helping you get ready!

This Roman fresco shows the beauty routine of some wealthy Roman women. A slave helps one lady with her hair. The jugs and pots probably contain perfumes and creams.

Roman clothes

Most Roman clothes were made from wool, but wealthy people wore clothes made from linen, cotton or even silk. The basic garment for men and boys was a short, belted tunic, but important Romans wore a toga in public. The toga was a long strip of cloth, wrapped around the body and draped over one shoulder. Women and girls dressed in a long, sleeveless dress known as a *stola*. On top of this they wore a large shawl, draped around the shoulders or looped over the head like a hood.

Hair and make-up

Looking good was very important to the Romans. Wealthy women often devoted several hours a day to their hair and make-up. Roman hairstyles could be very elaborate, and many women wore hairpieces or wigs. It was very fashionable for women to look pale, so servants applied a paste of powdered chalk to their mistress's face and arms. They darkened her eyebrows and eyelashes with soot and painted her lips with red plant dye.

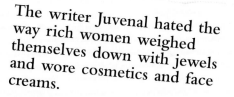

The writer Juvenal hated the way rich women weighed themselves down with jewels and wore cosmetics and face creams.

There is nothing a woman considers shameful, when she encircles her neck with green emeralds, and fastens huge pearls to her elongated ears.... Meanwhile she reeks of rich unguents [face creams] which stick to the lips of her unfortunate husband.

Juvenal, Satires, 1st century CE

A pair of gold earrings, dating from the second century BCE. Elaborate jewellery like this would only have been worn by the very rich. Poorer people wore jewellery made from bronze, copper and tin.

Jewellery

Wealthy Roman women wore gold earrings, necklaces and bracelets. Both men and women wore a lot of rings – often several on the same finger. In very rich families, even the children wore tiny gold rings.

AUDIENCE CHAMBER

Audience chamber

When you are changed and ready, make your way across to the audience chamber. This is the largest and grandest room in the villa. Notice the splendid columns supporting the ceiling, the beautifully painted walls, and the dramatic mosaic floors. Even though the chamber is so large, it is kept warm by a system of under-floor heating and by braziers filled with burning charcoal.

MOSAIC FLOORS – SEE PAGE 9

Furniture

The audience chamber of a large villa usually contained well-crafted furniture such as couches, benches and chairs. Guests were invited to enjoy snacks of fruit and wine laid out on small, low tables. The furniture in the audience chamber at Fishbourne was made from rare woods, bronze and ivory, and decorated with gold.

In this Roman carving, dating from the second century CE, a woman reclines on a couch and helps herself to snacks, while a pet dog looks on greedily!

16

Painted walls

The walls of Roman villas were usually decorated with colourful frescoes – paintings made by applying paint directly onto damp plaster. Many of these were plain blocks of colour or simple patterns. Often, walls were painted with architectural features, such as columns, and some frescoes showed elaborate scenes. The walls of some grand villas were decorated with stories of gods and goddesses, while frescoes in smaller villas often featured garden scenes or images of the farming year.

This impressive fresco comes from a large Roman town house in Herculaneum, southern Italy. Wealthy villa owners employed talented artists to decorate their walls with graceful figures such as these.

The walls of Emperor Nero's Golden Villa were painted by an artist called Amulius. Pliny describes an example of the artist's work:

By this artist there was a [painting of the goddess] Minerva, which had the appearance of always looking at the spectators, from whatever point it was viewed.

Pliny the Younger, Letters, 1st century CE

Under-floor heating

The homes of wealthy Romans were kept warm by a kind of under-floor heating known as a *hypocaust*. Hot air, warmed by a furnace in the basement, spread through the house along brick channels under the floors. Sometimes the floors became so hot that people had to wear wooden-soled sandals to protect their feet. The slaves who stoked the furnace often collapsed from the heat.

17

BATH-HOUSE

After meeting up with the other guests, it's time to relax and enjoy some free time before dinner. So why not head off to the bath-house? This private leisure complex contains an open-air exercise yard and three linked rooms: a hot room (*caldarium*), a warm room (*tepidarium*) and a cold room (*frigidarium*).

Bath-house

This is the *tepidarium* in the public baths at the Roman town of Herculaneum. In the public baths, groups of people bathed together, but men and women had separate sessions.

Warm and hot rooms

A visit to a Roman bath-house began by undressing in the *tepidarium*. The bathers lay on tables while slaves covered them with oil and gave them a relaxing massage. Next, they walked through to the *caldarium*. This room was heated by a *hypocaust* and was very hot. Once the bathers had developed a healthy sweat, slaves would scrape the oil, sweat and dirt off their bodies with a curved metal scraper, known as a *strigil*.

UNDER-FLOOR HEATING – SEE PAGE 17

Cold plunge

When the bathers were thoroughly clean, they would take a plunge in the pool in the *tepidarium*, then move on to the *frigidarium* for a splash in ice-cold water. This might be followed by a brisk run in the exercise yard. After this exercise session, people might return to the bathing rooms again, usually finishing with another cold plunge.

This mosaic decorated the wall of the *frigidarium* at a public baths in Sicily. It shows a man dressing, helped by two attendants.

Public baths were very popular in Roman times, but not everyone enjoyed them! Here is the writer Seneca's complaint:

I live over a public bath-house. Just imagine every kind of annoying noise! The sturdy gentleman does his exercise with lead weights and I can hear him grunt ... there's also the racket of the man who loves to hear his own voice in the bath and the chap who dives in with lots of noise and splashing.

Seneca the Younger, letter to a friend, 1st century CE

Public baths

Wealthy Romans had their own private bath-houses, but most Romans went to the public baths. These massive complexes contained several pools, a massage room and an exercise yard. The larger public baths also had a library and beautiful gardens. The baths were usually open from mid-morning to sunset every day. The Romans believed that it was important to stay clean and take regular exercise, so the baths were very cheap and children were let in free.

LIBRARY

After your exercise in the bath-house, you may like to spend some quiet time in the library, reading or writing letters. The library has hundreds of texts, written on parchment scrolls. These are stacked on wooden shelves, which are divided into square compartments. Luckily, you won't have to search for the scroll you want on your own. The villa's librarian is there to help you. He will also provide you with all the materials you need for writing.

Library

Reading and writing

Wealthy Romans were very well educated and loved to read for pleasure. Boys and girls were sent to school at the age of seven, where they learnt reading, writing and arithmetic. By the time they were ten years old, they were reading the works of the great authors in Latin and Greek. Girls left school at 11, but boys could continue to secondary school, where they studied Greek and Roman literature, mathematics, history, geography and music.

Some girls from rich families were educated at home by a tutor. This fresco shows a young girl holding a writing tablet and a metal stylus.

Roman readers had a wide range of texts to choose from. They could enjoy adventure stories, legends of the gods, and poetry. They could read plays in Latin or Greek, and they could study works of philosophy, history, geography and mathematics.

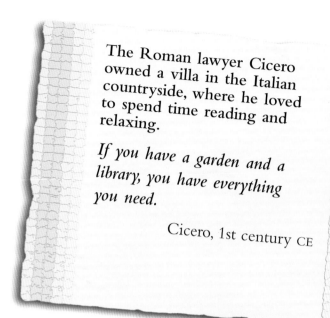

The Roman lawyer Cicero owned a villa in the Italian countryside, where he loved to spend time reading and relaxing.

If you have a garden and a library, you have everything you need.

Cicero, 1st century CE

Writing materials

The Romans used different materials for different kinds of writing. For unimportant texts, people often wrote on a wax tablet, using a pointed metal stick called a stylus. The tablet could then be melted down and used again. Sometimes they wrote with pen and ink on cheap, thin slices of wood. Important documents were written on scrolls of papyrus, a kind of paper made from reeds, which were imported from Egypt.

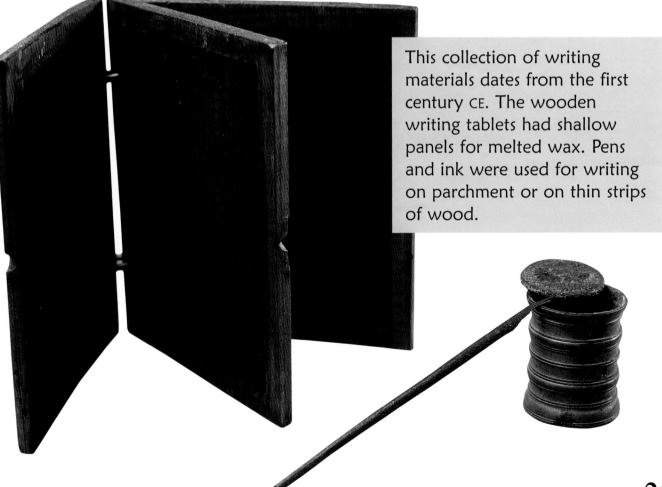

This collection of writing materials dates from the first century CE. The wooden writing tablets had shallow panels for melted wax. Pens and ink were used for writing on parchment or on thin strips of wood.

DINING ROOM

In the evening, you are invited to join your hosts for a special banquet. The dining room, or *triclinium*, is a long, narrow room with three couches arranged in a U-shape around some low tables. Take your place at the feast by stretching out on one of the couches. Wash your hands in the bowl of perfumed water brought by one of the household slaves. Then prepare yourself for a long evening – you can expect to eat at least six courses!

Dining room

Roman banquets

A Roman banquet started with a few cold courses, such as eggs, raw vegetables and fish. This was followed by the main courses, which were very rich and usually smothered in sauces. A typical menu for a banquet could include roast swan or deer, giant snails in garlic, and dormice served in honey sauce. These dishes were not consumed using knives and forks – guests ate with their fingers.

This fresco from Herculaneum in southern Italy shows some guests enjoying a banquet. On the left, a slave removes the shoes of a new guest while another slave offers him a cup of wine.

Creative cuisine

Roman cooks liked to show off their skill by disguising one type of food as another. They made swans from pastry and even disguised pigs to look like fish. Some cooks served up a dish that looked like a bird's nest filled with eggs. The nest was made from pastry and the eggs were made from sausage meat.

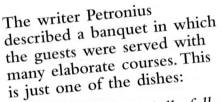

ROMAN FOOD AND COOKING – SEE PAGES 24–27

This silver jug was made in the first century BCE and is decorated with scenes of gods and goddesses. Jugs and dishes made from gold, silver and glass were used for serving wine and food at grand banquets.

The writer Petronius described a banquet in which the guests were served with many elaborate courses. This is just one of the dishes:

A wild pig with its belly full of live thrushes, quinces [a kind of fruit] stuck with thorns to look like sea urchins, and roast pork carved into models of fish, song birds and a goose.

Petronius, Satyricon, 1st century CE

Entertainments

During a banquet, guests were entertained by musicians, dancers, poets and clowns. Roman musicians played on flutes, tambourines and stringed instruments called lyres. Dancers clicked castanets to beat out the rhythm of their lively dances. Often, the most important dish in the banquet was carried into the dining room in a grand procession, accompanied by slaves playing flutes and dancing.

KITCHEN

Kitchen

During your stay, why not take a look inside the villa's kitchen? Roman kitchens are dark, hot and smoky. They are also very noisy and full of people. Inside the kitchen you will see many slaves at work – making pastry, chopping vegetables and grinding spices. Some slaves will be roasting meat on a spit over the fire, while others will be stirring pots on the stove. You may also see a large iron cauldron, hanging on chains over the fire.

This bronze cauldron dates from the second century CE. Poor people cooked bean stew in cauldrons like these.

Cooking equipment

The Romans cooked their food in bronze saucepans and earthenware pots. They had spoons and knives of all sizes, but no forks. They also had graters and strainers, and ground up their spices with a stone pestle and mortar. Roman stoves had panels filled with red-hot charcoal. The pots and pans were placed on iron racks above the charcoal.

Roman meals

Poorer Romans and slaves had to survive on very basic food, such as bread, porridge and bean stew, but wealthy Romans enjoyed a varied diet. Their day began with a light breakfast of bread with honey and fruit. Lunch was a cold meal of eggs, fish and vegetables. The evening meal usually included roast poultry or fish, served in a rich sauce. Roman sauces included powerful spices such as ginger, cumin and cardamom. They were often sweetened with honey and thickened with flour or crumbled pastry.

A Roman cookery book, known simply as *Apicius*, contains many recipes for fancy sauces. One of the recipes ends with this statement:

No one at table will know what he is eating.

Apicius, 4th century CE

Eating out

Not all Romans ate at home. In the cities, most people lived in apartments, which were made mainly from wood. It was forbidden to light fires in these buildings in case they burnt down. For this reason, people bought all their food from stalls in the street. These fast-food stalls sold a range of hot food, such as pies, sausages and stews. The stalls also sold wine, which the Romans drank with all their meals. Most people mixed their wine with water. Wine mixed with honey and spices was also popular.

The ruins of a tavern in a city street in Herculaneum, southern Italy. People living in towns brought hot snacks from roadside stalls and taverns.

STOREHOUSE

Near the kitchen is the storehouse, a large, cool building where the villa's food is kept. On the floor you see amphorae (tall pottery jars) holding olive oil and wine. There are baskets filled with spices and nuts, and barrels containing salted meat and fish. Joints of smoked bacon hang from the ceiling, and the walls are covered with bunches of herbs and strings of onion and garlic. The shelves are stacked with cheeses and jars of pickled fruit.

Storehouse

Flour for bread

All the villa's provisions were kept in the storehouse, including sacks of flour to supply the villa with bread. The flour was ground by the mill in the centre of the courtyard. A donkey, harnessed to the grindstone, walked around in circles, turning the stone to grind the wheat into flour. Slaves in the nearby bakehouse made the flour into bread and baked it in the oven.

Roman amphorae all had the same basic design. Their twin handles made them easy to transport, while their narrow necks and thick sides allowed their contents to remain fresh and cool.

26

Food from the empire

Most of the food used in a Roman British villa came from the villa's farm, but some food was imported from other parts of the Roman Empire. Oil, wine, olives and dates came from Italy or Greece, while spices, such as cumin, cardamom and pepper, arrived in merchant ships from the east. One very popular imported food was *liquamen*, a spicy sauce made from fermented fish. It was made in Spain and sent all over the Roman Empire.

VILLA FARMS –
SEE PAGES 6–7

This carving shows a Roman merchant ship, loaded with wine barrels. Merchants used rowing boats like this for short river journeys, but they also had much larger sailing ships for sea voyages.

Cato gives some tough advice on how to run a profitable farm:

You must take stock and order to be sold whatever will be surplus. You must sell oil, wine and grain; sell aging oxen, wool, hides, an old cart, old iron tools, an old slave, and anything else surplus. The master has to be a selling man, not a buying man.

Cato, On Agriculture,
1st century BCE

Food for market

Once the villa's storehouse was full, any extra food could be sent to market. Servants from the villa travelled to local markets with their grain, meat, wool and other farm produce. Trading food over long distances was made possible because the Romans built excellent roads. Roman merchants also had sturdy ships that could make lengthy voyages. Roman merchant ships travelled as far north as Scotland and as far east as India.

27

SLAVES' DORMITORY

Slaves' dormitory

Close to the storehouse is the slaves' dormitory. Should you enter, you will find a dark, bare room very different from the rooms in the main villa. It has an earth floor and bare walls, and is divided by wooden walls into small cubicles. Each cubicle has a very basic bed – a wooden shelf covered by a straw mattress. The slaves keep their few possessions under their bed.

Life as a slave

Roman slaves were completely owned by their master or mistress. Owners could decide how to punish their slaves and some villas had a prison for disobedient slaves. Some slaves were treated cruelly and worked very long hours. Other slaves received much better treatment. They were properly fed and clothed, and their owners made sure that they were cared for when they were sick. When they became too old to work, most slaves stayed on in their owner's villa and were looked after for the rest of their lives.

A Roman slave waits on his master. Many slaves came from distant parts of the empire, where they had been captured as prisoners of war.

28

Trusted slaves

Some household slaves remained with the same family for generations. These trusted slaves were seen as part of their owner's family. They had their own rooms within the villa, rather than living in dormitories. Sometimes, the children of a trusted slave were brought up with the owner's children, sharing their games and even their lessons. These well-educated slaves might later work in the villa as librarians or tutors.

ROMAN EDUCATION –
SEE PAGES 20–21

In this letter to a friend, Pliny explains that his freedman Zosimus is sick, and asks his friend to allow Zosimus to visit his farm for health reasons:

He is a good, honest fellow, attentive in his services and well-read. He is indeed endeared to me by the ties of a long affection. For this reason I intend to send him to your farm having frequently heard you mention its healthy air.

Pliny the Younger, Letters, 1st century CE

Becoming free

Slavery was not always for life. Sometimes, an owner freed a loyal slave as a reward for many years' service. Other owners gave their slaves small amounts of money, which the slaves could gradually save up to buy their freedom. Freed slaves were given the status of 'freedmen'. This allowed them to buy a house and even to keep slaves of their own. However, many freedmen continued to work for their masters.

This Roman carving shows a master freeing his slave. In this ceremony, the slave wears the pointed cap of liberty to show that he is now a freedman.

29

TIMELINE

BCE

c. 750 The Latin people found the city of Rome.

c. 510 The Roman Republic begins. (During the Republic, the Romans are ruled by a group of politicians, known as the senate.)

c. 265 The Romans have gained control of the whole of Italy.

133 Rome gains control of Asia.

73 The gladiator Spartacus leads a revolt of slaves.

63 The Romans conquer lands in the Middle East.

55 Julius Caesar invades Britain, but withdraws the following year.

44 Julius Caesar is assassinated because he tries to seize too much power.

27 Augustus becomes the first Roman emperor.

CE

43 The Romans conquer Britain.
Grain stores are built at Fishbourne, in southern Britain, as a supply base for the Roman army.

c. 60 A small villa is built at Fishbourne, including a bath-house.

c. 73 The small villa at Fishbourne is demolished and building work begins on a grand villa, incorporating the original bath-house. It is probably built for Cogidubnus, a pro-Roman British chieftain.

79 The Colosseum is built in Rome.
Mount Vesuvius erupts in western Italy, burying the town of Pompeii.

101 Emperor Trajan starts to win land in Dacia (present-day Eastern Europe).

117 The Roman Empire reaches its largest size.

c. 120 Building work begins on Emperor Hadrian's villa at Tivoli in Italy.

122 Hadrian's wall is built in northern Britain to keep out invaders.

200 Barbarian tribes start to attack the empire's borders.

270 The Romans start to abandon parts of the empire.

313 Emperor Constantine allows Christians to worship freely.

367 Barbarian tribes begin to set up kingdoms inside the Roman Empire.

383 The Romans start to withdraw from Britain.

395 The Roman Empire splits into two parts – east and west.

455 Barbarians invade Italy and attack Rome.

476 The Roman Empire collapses.

GLOSSARY

amphora A large jar with two handles, used for storing wine and oil.

atrium The entrance hall of a Roman villa.

braziers Metal baskets filled with logs or coal for burning.

caldarium The hot room in a bath-house.

castanets A musical instrument, made from a pair of wooden or metal shells joined on one edge by string. They are held in the hand and used to produce rhythmic clicks.

dormitory A large building with many beds, where people sleep.

fermented Turned into alcohol.

field hands Farm labourers, who work in the fields.

foreman The person in charge of a group of workers.

fresco A kind of painting that is applied directly onto a wall while the plaster is still wet. It is very hardwearing and keeps its brilliant colours.

frigidarium The cold room in a bath-house.

geometric Shaped like a square, a triangle or a rectangle.

hypocaust An under-floor heating system.

impluvium A long, rectangular pool in the centre of an atrium.

import Bring foreign goods into a country.

lararium A shrine to the household spirits.

lares Household spirits.

liquamen A very strong sauce made from fermented fish.

lyre A musical instrument that looks like a small harp.

mosaic A pattern or picture made up of small pieces of coloured stone.

papyrus Fine paper made from reeds that grew in ancient Egypt.

peristyle A covered walkway around a garden or a courtyard.

pestle and mortar A bowl and grinder, used for grinding up spices and other foods.

Saturnalia A feast to celebrate midwinter.

shrine A place where holy objects are kept. Shrines can be small buildings, altars, or cupboards.

stola A long robe worn by Roman women.

strigil A curved stick used for scraping oil and dirt from the skin.

stylus A stick with a pointed end, used for writing on a wax tablet.

tepidarium The warm room in a bath-house.

tesserae Tiles used in a mosaic.

toga A long piece of cloth, worn draped around the body.

triclinium A dining room.

FURTHER INFORMATION

Books

Ancient Roman Homes by Brian Williams (Heinemann Library, 2002)

Fishbourne: A Day in a Roman Palace by Tony Triggs (Hodder Wayland, 1997)

Fishbourne Roman Palace: An illustrated family guide by David Rudkin (Sussex Archaeological Society, 2000)

History from Buildings: Roman Britain by Alex Woolf (Franklin Watts, 2006)

Inside Story: A Roman Villa by Jacqueline Morley and John James (Macdonald, 1996)

The Roman World by Fiona Chandler, Sam Taplin and Jane Bingham (Usborne, 2001)

Websites

http://www.brims.co.uk/romans/
A fun, interactive site on Roman life. It includes sections on Roman towns and homes, food and farming.

http://www.villa-rustica.de/indexe.html
A guided tour around a large Roman villa in Germany, with 27 stops.

http://sights.seindal.dk/sight/456_Villa_Romana_del_Casale.html
A website on a Roman villa on the island of Sicily. The villa has excellent mosaics.

http://www.britainexpress.com/architecture/roman-villas.htm
A brief survey of Roman villas in Britain, with a list of villas to visit.

INDEX